Onigiri with a Twist Cookbook

Modern Onigiri Recipe Twists

BY

Stephanie Sharp

Copyright © 2020 by Stephanie Sharp

License Notes

Copyright 2020 by Stephanie Sharp All rights reserved.

No part of this Book may be transmitted or reproduced into any format for any means without the proper permission of the Author. This includes electronic or mechanical methods, photocopying or printing.

The Reader assumes all risk when following any of the guidelines or ideas written as they are purely suggestion and for informational purposes. The Author has taken every precaution to ensure accuracy of the work but bears no responsibility if damages occur due to a misinterpretation of suggestions.

wwwwwwwwwwwwwwwwwwwwwwwww

Table of Contents

Introduction 6

Tropical Onigiri Cone 8

Sake Onigiri Nori 11

Yukari Onigiri 14

Spicy Tuna Onigiri 16

Tori-Soboro Onigiri 19

Shrimp (Ebi) Tail Onigiri 22

Whale Meat Onigiri 24

BBQ Beef Onigiri 26

Spicy Tuna Onigiri Bowl 29

Dragon Onigiri 31

Tako (Octopus) Onigiri 34

Scallop Onigiri 37

Yellowtail Onigiri 40

Rainbow Onigiri 42

Fried Shrimp Onigiri 45

Puffer Fish Onigiri 48

Smoked Turkey Onigiri 50

California Onigiri Cone 52

Philadelphia Onigiri 55

Tuna (Maguro) Onigiri 58

Mackerel (Saba) Onigiri 60

Horse Mackerel (Aji) Onigiri 62

Bacon Onigiri 64

Sea Urchin Onigiri 66

California Onigiri 68

Fatty Tuna Onigiri 71

Boston Onigiri 73

Seattle Onigiri 76

Smoked Salmon Onigiri 79

Teriyaki chicken Onigiri 81

Conclusion 84

About the Author 85

Author's Afterthoughts 86

Introduction

Did you know that Onigiri simply translates to rice balls in Japan?

That's right! Rice balls are called onigiri in most of Japan. The regions that don't refer to them as Omusubi. They were named from the preface of how they are made, i.e onigiri, formed from 'nigiri' that means to grip and 'musubi' that literally means to bond or tie something.

Onigiri is often compared to sushi and even Japanese sandwiches based on the flavors. It is often enjoyed for lunch, on picnics and evenlight dinners. There are so many different flavors and filings for you to enjoy, mix and experiment with that your palate will be entertained for days. So, let's not delay any further, it's time for onigiri.

Tropical Onigiri Cone

This exotic modern onigiri cone will leave you to refresh and impressed.

Yields: 3 cones

Time Needed: 30 minutes

Ingredients:

- Cooked Plain rice (1 cups)
- Shiso Leaves (6)
- Mango (1, seeded, and julienned)
- Pineapple (1/2, thinly sliced)
- Crab Meat (1 Cup, shredded)
- Nori (3 sheets)
- Kewpie Mayo (2 tbsp.)
- Tobiko (1 tbsp.)
- Sesame Seeds (to sprinkle for garnish)

Directions:

1. Place your nori on a flat surface with the silkier side facing down.

2. Top with 4 tablespoons of your Plain rice. Carefully wet your palms with water then proceed to rub your palms with a dash of salt.

3. Spread the rice evenly over the left side of the nori sheet. Once spread evenly sprinkle with sesame seeds.

4. Top with two Shiso leaves on a bias, followed by some mango, crab, a slice of pineapple, and a teaspoon of kewpie mayo.

5. Placing your index and middle fingers in front of your filling to hold it in, position your thumbs below the nori sheet and roll the nori from the left-hand corner to the top right end forming a cone.

6. Use a grain of rice to stick your nori together.

7. Top with Tobiko, and sesame seeds

8. Repeat with all three sheets.

9. Serve and Enjoy!

Sake Onigiri Nori

Sake, the Japanese name for Salmon, is a popular Sashimi fish used in both sushi and onigiri.

Serves: 8

Time: 30 minutes

Ingredients:

- Cooked Plain rice (1½ cups)
- Fresh Salmon (4 oz., sashimi grade, thinly sliced lengthwise)
- Cucumber (4oz, diced)
- Fresh Crab Meat (4oz., sashimi grade, diced)
- Sesame Oil (1/2 tsp.)
- Nori (1 sheet, cut into strips)
- Sesame Seeds (2 tbsp.)
- Salt (enough to fill a small bowl, can put back what is not used)

Directions:

1. Combine crab meat, cucumber, and sesame oil in a medium bowl.

2. Set your rice next to you, a second bowl next to it with salt, an empty bowl in front of you and finally another large bowl with water.

3. Add a heaping spoonful of rice to the empty bowl (as much as needed for the size of onigiri you want to achieve).

4. Dip your hands into your water bowl, then rub your wet hands with a dash of salt.

5. Press the serving of rice into your palm to create a small well.

6. Add in your fillings combined in step one, then push it lightly into the rice.

7. Form the rice into a ball of triangle (based on preference).

8. Wrap your onigiri with a strip of nori then dip into sesame seeds if you so desire or serve. Enjoy!

Yukari Onigiri

If you love the taste of rich Japanese fish then this one is a must try.

Yields: 6 pieces

Time: 30 Minutes

Ingredients:

- Cooked Plain rice (1½ cups)
- Fresh Yukari (6 oz., thinly sliced)
- Sesame Oil (2 tbsp.)

Directions:

1. Set your rice next to you, a second bowl next to it with salt, an empty bowl in front of you and finally another large bowl with water.

2. Add a heaping spoonful of rice to the empty bowl (as much as needed for the size of onigiri you want to achieve).

3. Dip your hands into your water bowl, then rub your wet hands with a dash of salt.

4. Press the serving of rice into your palm to create a small well.

5. Form the rice into a ball of triangle (based on preference).

6. Wrap your onigiri with a strip of whale then drizzle with sesame oil if you so desire or serve. Enjoy!

Spicy Tuna Onigiri

A spicy combination of fresh tuna, nori, and Plain rice.

Yields: 8 pieces

Time: 30 minutes

Ingredients:

- Cooked Plain rice (1½ cups)
- Fresh Tuna (4 oz., sashimi grade, minced)
- Sriracha Sauce (3 tsp.)
- Green Onion (1 tsp, chopped)
- Sesame Oil (1/2 tsp.)
- Nori (1 sheet, halved)
- Sesame Seeds (2 tbsp.)
- Spicy Mayo (optional for garnish/dipping)

Directions:

1. Combine minced tuna, green onions, sesame oil, and sriracha sauce.

2. Set your rice next to you, a second bowl next to it with salt, an empty bowl in front of you and finally another large bowl with water.

3. Add a heaping spoonful of rice to the empty bowl (as much as needed for the size of onigiri you want to achieve).

4. Dip your hands into your water bowl, then rub your wet hands with a dash of salt.

5. Press the serving of rice into your palm to create a small well.

6. Add in your fillings combined in step one, then push it lightly into the rice.

7. Form the rice into a ball of triangle (based on preference).

8. Wrap your onigiri with a strip of nori then dip into sesame seeds if you so desire or serve. Enjoy!

Tori-Soboro Onigiri

If you are big on strong Japanese flavors this onigiri recipe is definitely for you.

Yields: 8 pieces

Time: 30 minutes

Ingredients:

- Cooked Plain rice (1½ cups)
- Tori-Soboro (4 oz., minced)
- Sriracha Sauce (3 tsp.)
- Green Onion (1 tsp, chopped)
- Sesame Oil (1/2 tsp.)
- Nori (1 sheet, halved)
- Sesame Seeds (2 tbsp.)
- Spicy Mayo (optional for garnish/dipping)

Directions:

1. Combine Tori-Soboro, green onions, sesame oil, and sriracha sauce.

2. Set your rice next to you, a second bowl next to it with salt, an empty bowl in front of you and finally another large bowl with water.

3. Add a heaping spoonful of rice to the empty bowl (as much as needed for the size of onigiri you want to achieve).

4. Dip your hands into your water bowl, then rub your wet hands with a dash of salt.

5. Press the serving of rice into your palm to create a small well.

6. Add in your fillings combined in step one, then push it lightly into the rice.

7. Form the rice into a ball of triangle (based on preference).

8. Wrap your onigiri with a strip of nori then dip into sesame seeds if you so desire or serve. Enjoy!

Shrimp (Ebi) Tail Onigiri

Shrimp lovers will absolutely love this onigiri!

Yields: 6 Pieces

Time Needed: 30 min

Ingredients:

- Cooked Plain rice (1½ cups)
- Fresh Shrimp Tail Meat (6 oz., large, seasoned with salt and lemon zest)
- Sesame Oil (2 tbsp.)

Directions:

1. Set your rice next to you, a second bowl next to it with salt, an empty bowl in front of you and finally another large bowl with water.

2. Add a heaping spoonful of rice to the empty bowl (as much as needed for the size of onigiri you want to achieve).

3. Dip your hands into your water bowl, then rub your wet hands with a dash of salt.

4. Press the serving of rice into your palm to create a small well.

5. Form the rice into a ball of triangle (based on preference).

6. Wrap your onigiri with a shrimp tail then dip into sesame seeds if you so desire or serve. Enjoy!

Whale Meat Onigiri

A delicious, yet exotic onigiri.

Yields: 6 pieces

Time: 30 Minutes

Ingredients:

- Cooked Plain rice (1½ cups)
- Fresh Whale Meat (6 oz., thinly sliced)
- Sesame Oil (2 tbsp.)

Directions:

1. Set your rice next to you, a second bowl next to it with salt, an empty bowl in front of you and finally another large bowl with water.

2. Add a heaping spoonful of rice to the empty bowl (as much as needed for the size of onigiri you want to achieve).

3. Dip your hands into your water bowl, then rub your wet hands with a dash of salt.

4. Press the serving of rice into your palm to create a small well.

5. Form the rice into a ball of triangle (based on preference).

6. Wrap your onigiri with a strip of whale then drizzle with sesame oil if you so desire or serve. Enjoy!

BBQ Beef Onigiri

BBQ beef and spicy mayo pairs well in this tasty onigiri recipe.

Yields: 8 pieces

Time: 30 minutes

Ingredients:

- Cooked Plain rice (1½ cups)
- BBQ beef (4 oz., minced)
- Spicy Mayo (3 tsp.)
- Green Onion (1 tsp, chopped)
- Sesame Oil (1/2 tsp.)
- Nori (1 sheet, halved)
- Sesame Seeds (2 tbsp.)
- Spicy Mayo (optional for garnish/dipping)

Directions:

1. Combine BBQ beef, green onions, sesame oil, and spicy mayo.

2. Set your rice next to you, a second bowl next to it with salt, an empty bowl in front of you and finally another large bowl with water.

3. Add a heaping spoonful of rice to the empty bowl (as much as needed for the size of onigiri you want to achieve).

4. Dip your hands into your water bowl, then rub your wet hands with a dash of salt.

5. Press the serving of rice into your palm to create a small well.

6. Add in your fillings combined in step one, then push it lightly into the rice.

7. Form the rice into a ball of triangle (based on preference).

8. Wrap your onigiri with a strip of nori then dip into sesame seeds if you so desire or serve. Enjoy!

Spicy Tuna Onigiri Bowl

All the pleasures of a spicy tuna onigiri in a bowl.

Ingredients:

- Cooked Plain rice (1½ cups)
- Fresh Tuna (4 oz., sashimi grade, minced)
- Cucumber (4oz, fine julienne)
- Carrot (4oz., fine julienne)
- Green Onion (1 tsp, chopped)
- Sesame Oil (1/2 tsp.)
- Sesame Seeds (2 tbsp.)
- Soy sauce (2 tsp.)

Directions:

1. Split your Plain rice into 2 medium bowls.

2. Top with your tuna, cucumber, carrot, and green onion.

3. Sprinkle with sesame seeds.

4. Top tuna with soy sauce.

5. Serve and enjoy!

Dragon Onigiri

A tasty combination of eel, cucumber, and caviar.

Yields: 6 pieces

Time: 30 minutes

Ingredients:

- Cooked Plain rice (1½ cups)
- Fresh Eel (4 oz., sashimi grade, thinly sliced lengthwise)
- Cucumber (4oz, diced)
- Caviar (2oz.)
- Sesame Oil (1/2 tsp.)
- Nori (1 sheet, halved)
- Sesame Seeds (2 tbsp.)

Directions:

1. Combine eel, cucumber, and sesame oil in a medium bowl.

2. Set your rice next to you, a second bowl next to it with salt, an empty bowl in front of you and finally another large bowl with water.

3. Add a heaping spoonful of rice to the empty bowl (as much as needed for the size of onigiri you want to achieve).

4. Dip your hands into your water bowl, then rub your wet hands with a dash of salt.

5. Press the serving of rice into your palm to create a small well.

6. Add in your fillings combined in step one, then push it lightly into the rice.

7. Form the rice into a ball of triangle (based on preference).

8. Wrap your onigiri with a strip of nori then dip into sesame seeds if you so desire or serve. Enjoy!

Tako (Octopus) Onigiri

A brilliant combination of Tako, the Japanese term for Octopus, and Plain rice.

Yields: 6 Pieces

Time: 30 min

Ingredients:

- Cooked Plain rice (1½ cups)
- Fresh Tako/Octopus (4 oz., sashimi grade, thinly sliced lengthwise)
- Perilla Leaves (12 leaves, washed)
- Sesame Oil (1/2 tsp.)

Directions:

1. Set your rice next to you, a second bowl next to it with salt, an empty bowl in front of you and finally another large bowl with water.

2. Add a heaping spoonful of rice to the empty bowl (as much as needed for the size of onigiri you want to achieve).

3. Dip your hands into your water bowl, then rub your wet hands with a dash of salt.

4. Press the serving of rice into your palm to create a small well.

5. Form the rice into a ball of triangle (based on preference).

6. Wrap your onigiri with a perilla leaf and Tako then dip into drizzle with sesame oil. Enjoy!

Scallop Onigiri

The delicacies of a scallop paired with the velocity of Plain rice.

Yields: 6

Time: 30 minutes

Ingredients:

- Cooked Plain rice (1½ cups)
- Fresh Scallop (6 oz., minced)
- Sesame Oil (2 tbsp.)

Directions:

1. Set your rice next to you, a second bowl next to it with salt, an empty bowl in front of you and finally another large bowl with water.

2. Add a heaping spoonful of rice to the empty bowl (as much as needed for the size of onigiri you want to achieve).

3. Dip your hands into your water bowl, then rub your wet hands with a dash of salt.

4. Press the serving of rice into your palm to create a small well.

5. Add in your scallop, then push it lightly into the rice.

6. Form the rice into a ball of triangle (based on preference).

7. Drizzle with sesame oil if you so desire then serve. Enjoy!

Yellowtail Onigiri

Plain rice topped with delicate yellowtail.

Yields: 6

Time: 30 minutes

Ingredients:

- Cooked Plain rice (1½ cups)
- Fresh Yellowtail (6 oz., thinly sliced)
- Sesame Oil (2 tbsp.)

Directions:

1. Set your rice next to you, a second bowl next to it with salt, an empty bowl in front of you and finally another large bowl with water.

2. Add a heaping spoonful of rice to the empty bowl (as much as needed for the size of onigiri you want to achieve).

3. Dip your hands into your water bowl, then rub your wet hands with a dash of salt.

4. Press the serving of rice into your palm to create a small well.

5. Form the rice into a ball of triangle (based on preference).

6. Wrap your onigiri with a strip of yellowtail then drizzle with sesame oil if you so desire or serve. Enjoy!

Rainbow Onigiri

A colorful burst of deliciousness that you just can't help but admire while you eat.

Yields: 6 Pieces

Time: 30 minutes

Ingredients:

- Cooked Plain rice (1½ cups, colored with spices)
- Fresh Salmon (4 oz., sashimi grade, thinly sliced lengthwise)
- Fresh Ahi Tuna (4 oz., sashimi grade, thinly sliced lengthwise)
- Cucumber (4oz, diced)
- Fresh Crab Meat (4oz., sashimi grade, minced)
- Sesame Oil (1/2 tsp.)
- Sriracha Sauce (3 tsp.)
- Nori (1 sheet, cut in strips)
- Sesame Seeds (2 tbsp.)

Directions:

1. Combine crab meat, cucumber, sriracha sauce, and sesame oil in a medium bowl.

2. Set your rice next to you, a second bowl next to it with salt, an empty bowl in front of you and finally another large bowl with water.

3. Add a heaping spoonful of rice to the empty bowl (as much as needed for the size of onigiri you want to achieve).

4. Dip your hands into your water bowl, then rub your wet hands with a dash of salt.

5. Press the serving of rice into your palm to create a small well.

6. Add in your fillings combined in step one, then push it lightly into the rice.

7. Form the rice into a ball of triangle (based on preference).

8. Wrap your onigiri with a strip of nori then dip into sesame seeds if you so desire or serve. Enjoy!

Fried Shrimp Onigiri

The magical combination of fried shrimp, avocado, and Plain rice.

Yields: 6 Pieces

Time: 30 minutes

Ingredients:

- Cooked Plain rice (1½ cups)
- Shrimp (4 oz., diced, fried)
- Salt (2 tsp.)
- Sesame Oil (1/2 tsp.)
- Nori (1 sheet, halved)
- Sesame Seeds (2 tbsp.)

Directions:

1. Combine fried shrimp, sesame oil, and salt in a medium bowl.

2. Set your rice next to you, a second bowl next to it with salt, an empty bowl in front of you and finally another large bowl with water.

3. Add a heaping spoonful of rice to the empty bowl (as much as needed for the size of onigiri you want to achieve).

4. Dip your hands into your water bowl, then rub your wet hands with a dash of salt.

5. Press the serving of rice into your palm to create a small well.

6. Add in your fillings combined in step one, then push it lightly into the rice.

7. Form the rice into a ball of triangle (based on preference).

8. Wrap your onigiri with a strip of nori then dip into sesame seeds if you so desire or serve. Enjoy!

Puffer Fish Onigiri

Again, another exotic dish that can be easily prepared.

Yields: 6 pieces

Time: 30 minutes

Ingredients:

- Cooked Plain rice (1½ cups)
- Fresh Pufferfish (6 oz., large thinly sliced)
- Sesame Oil (2 tbsp.)

Directions:

1. Set your rice next to you, a second bowl next to it with salt, an empty bowl in front of you and finally another large bowl with water.

2. Add a heaping spoonful of rice to the empty bowl (as much as needed for the size of onigiri you want to achieve).

3. Dip your hands into your water bowl, then rub your wet hands with a dash of salt.

4. Press the serving of rice into your palm to create a small well.

5. Form the rice into a ball of triangle (based on preference).

6. Wrap your onigiri with a strip of puffer fish then drizzle with sesame oil if you so desire or serve. Enjoy!

Smoked Turkey Onigiri

This delicious onigiri twist will make you fall for smoked turkey.

Yields: 6

Time: 30 minutes

Ingredients:

- Cooked Plain rice (1½ cups)
- Fresh Smoked turkey (6 oz., thinly sliced)
- Sesame Oil (2 tbsp.)

Directions:

1. Set your rice next to you, a second bowl next to it with salt, an empty bowl in front of you and finally another large bowl with water.

2. Add a heaping spoonful of rice to the empty bowl (as much as needed for the size of onigiri you want to achieve).

3. Dip your hands into your water bowl, then rub your wet hands with a dash of salt.

4. Press the serving of rice into your palm to create a small well.

5. Form the rice into a ball of triangle (based on preference).

6. Wrap your onigiri with a strip of smoked turkey then drizzle with sesame oil if you so desire or serve. Enjoy!

California Onigiri Cone

A onigiri meal that you can hold in your hand.

Yields: 3 cones

Time Needed: 30 minutes

Ingredients:

- Cooked Plain rice (1 cups)
- Shiso Leaves (6)
- Japanese Cucumber (1, seeded, and julienned)
- Avocado (1/2, thinly sliced)
- Crab Meat (1 Cup, shredded)
- Nori (3 sheets)
- Kewpie Mayo (2 tbsp.)
- Tobiko (1 tbsp.)
- Sesame Seeds (to sprinkle for garnish)

Directions:

1. Place your nori on a flat surface with the silkier side facing down.

2. Top with 4 tablespoons of your Plain rice. Carefully wet your palms with water then proceed to rub your palms with a dash of salt.

3. Spread the rice evenly over the left side of the nori sheet. Once spread evenly sprinkle with sesame seeds.

4. Top with two Shiso leaves on a bias, followed by some cucumber, crab, a slice of avocado, and a teaspoon of kewpie mayo.

5. Placing your index and middle fingers in front of your filling to hold it in, position your thumbs below the nori sheet and roll the nori from the left-hand corner to the top right end forming a cone.

6. Use a grain of rice to stick your nori together.

7. Top with Tobiko, and sesame seeds

8. Repeat with all three sheets.

9. Serve and Enjoy!

Philadelphia Onigiri

A dazzling combination of salmon and cream cheese.

Yields: 6

Time: 30 minutes

Ingredients:

- Cooked Plain rice (1½ cups)
- Cucumber (4 oz., diced)
- Avocado (1/2, diced)
- Fresh Salmon (4oz., diced)
- Onion (1, small, chopped)
- Cream Cheese (1/4 cup., diced)
- Nori (1 sheet, halved)
- Sesame Seeds (2 tbsp.)

Directions:

1. Combine salmon, cucumber, avocado, onion, and cream cheese in a medium bowl.

2. Set your rice next to you, a second bowl next to it with salt, an empty bowl in front of you and finally another large bowl with water.

3. Add a heaping spoonful of rice to the empty bowl (as much as needed for the size of onigiri you want to achieve).

4. Dip your hands into your water bowl, then rub your wet hands with a dash of salt.

5. Press the serving of rice into your palm to create a small well.

6. Add in your fillings combined in step one, then push it lightly into the rice.

7. Form the rice into a ball of triangle (based on preference).

8. Wrap your onigiri with a strip of nori then dip into sesame seeds if you so desire or serve. Enjoy!

Tuna (Maguro) Onigiri

There's nothing tastier than a fresh slice of tuna paired with Plain rice.

Yields: 6 Pieces

Time: 30 Minutes

Ingredients:

- Cooked Plain rice (1½ cups)
- Fresh Tuna Meat (6 oz., large, sashimi grade, thinly sliced)
- Sesame Oil (2 tbsp.)

Directions:

1. Set your rice next to you, a second bowl next to it with salt, an empty bowl in front of you and finally another large bowl with water.

2. Add a heaping spoonful of rice to the empty bowl (as much as needed for the size of onigiri you want to achieve).

3. Dip your hands into your water bowl, then rub your wet hands with a dash of salt.

4. Press the serving of rice into your palm to create a small well.

5. Form the rice into a ball of triangle (based on preference).

6. Wrap your onigiri with a strip of tuna then drizzle with sesame oil if you so desire or serve. Enjoy!

Mackerel (Saba) Onigiri

That's right! Mackerel can, in fact, be used to make onigiri. Here's a delicious recipe showing how.

Yields: 6 pieces

Time: 30 minutes

Ingredients:

- Cooked Plain rice (1½ cups)
- Fresh Mackerel Meat (6 oz., large, sashimi grade, thinly sliced)
- Sesame Oil (2 tbsp.)

Directions:

1. Set your rice next to you, a second bowl next to it with salt, an empty bowl in front of you and finally another large bowl with water.

2. Add a heaping spoonful of rice to the empty bowl (as much as needed for the size of onigiri you want to achieve).

3. Dip your hands into your water bowl, then rub your wet hands with a dash of salt.

4. Press the serving of rice into your palm to create a small well.

5. Form the rice into a ball of triangle (based on preference).

6. Wrap your onigiri with a strip of mackerel then drizzle with sesame oil if you so desire or serve. Enjoy!

Horse Mackerel (Aji) Onigiri

A delicious fish from the Atlantic, that when eaten at its freshest peak is utterly delicious.

Yields 6 pieces

Time: 30 Minutes

Ingredients:

- Cooked Plain rice (1½ cups)
- Fresh Horse Mackerel Meat (6 oz., large, sashimi grade, thinly sliced)
- Sesame Oil (2 tbsp.)

Directions:

1. Set your rice next to you, a second bowl next to it with salt, an empty bowl in front of you and finally another large bowl with water.

2. Add a heaping spoonful of rice to the empty bowl (as much as needed for the size of onigiri you want to achieve).

3. Dip your hands into your water bowl, then rub your wet hands with a dash of salt.

4. Press the serving of rice into your palm to create a small well.

5. Form the rice into a ball of triangle (based on preference).

6. Wrap your onigiri with a strip of horse mackerel then drizzle with sesame oil if you so desire or serve. Enjoy!

Bacon Onigiri

Enjoy our American – Japanese fusion with this Bacon Onigiri.

Yields: 6

Time: 30 minutes

Ingredients:

- Cooked Plain rice (1½ cups)
- Crispy Bacon (6 oz., thinly sliced)
- Sesame Oil (2 tbsp.)

Directions:

1. Set your rice next to you, a second bowl next to it with salt, an empty bowl in front of you and finally another large bowl with water.

2. Add a heaping spoonful of rice to the empty bowl (as much as needed for the size of onigiri you want to achieve).

3. Dip your hands into your water bowl, then rub your wet hands with a dash of salt.

4. Press the serving of rice into your palm to create a small well.

5. Form the rice into a ball of triangle (based on preference).

6. Wrap your onigiri with a strip of bacon then drizzle with sesame oil if you so desire or serve. Enjoy!

Sea Urchin Onigiri

A new and interesting way to enjoy sea urchin.

Yields: 6 pieces

Time: 30 minutes

Ingredients:

- Cooked Plain rice (1½ cups)
- Fresh Sea Urchin (6 oz., thinly sliced)
- Sesame Oil (2 tbsp.)

Directions:

1. Set your rice next to you, a second bowl next to it with salt, an empty bowl in front of you and finally another large bowl with water.

2. Add a heaping spoonful of rice to the empty bowl (as much as needed for the size of onigiri you want to achieve).

3. Dip your hands into your water bowl, then rub your wet hands with a dash of salt.

4. Press the serving of rice into your palm to create a small well.

5. Form the rice into a ball of triangle (based on preference).

6. Wrap your onigiri with a strip of sea urchin then drizzle with sesame oil if you so desire or serve. Enjoy!

California Onigiri

A deliciously popular onigiri roll and an absolute crowd pleaser!

Yields: 8 pieces

Time: 30 minutes

Ingredients:

- Cooked Plain rice (1½ cups)
- Fresh Crab Meat (1 can season with salt and lemon zest)
- Nori (2 sheets, roasted, cut into strips)
- Avocado (1, diced)
- Cucumber (1, diced)
- Sesame Seeds (2 tbsp.)

Directions:

1. Combine crab meat, avocado, and cucumber.

2. Set your rice next to you, a second bowl next to it with salt, an empty bowl in front of you and finally another large bowl with water.

3. Add a heaping spoonful of rice to the empty bowl (as much as needed for the size of onigiri you want to achieve).

4. Dip your hands into your water bowl, then rub your wet hands with a dash of salt.

5. Press the serving of rice into your palm to create a small well.

6. Add in your fillings combined in step one, then push it lightly into the rice.

7. Form the rice into a ball of triangle (based on preference).

8. Wrap your onigiri with a strip of nori then dip into sesame seeds if you so desire or serve. Enjoy!

Fatty Tuna Onigiri

Indulge in the smooth, silky pleasure of fatty tuna, alongside Plain rice.

Yields: 6 pieces

Time: 30 minutes

Ingredients:

- Cooked Plain rice (1½ cups)
- Fresh Otorro Tuna Meat (6 oz., large, sashimi grade, thinly sliced)
- Sesame Oil (2 tbsp.)

Directions:

1. Set your rice next to you, a second bowl next to it with salt, an empty bowl in front of you and finally another large bowl with water.

2. Add a heaping spoonful of rice to the empty bowl (as much as needed for the size of onigiri you want to achieve).

3. Dip your hands into your water bowl, then rub your wet hands with a dash of salt.

4. Press the serving of rice into your palm to create a small well.

5. Form the rice into a ball of triangle (based on preference).

6. Wrap your onigiri with a strip of Otorro tuna then drizzle with sesame oil if you so desire or serve. Enjoy!

Boston Onigiri

Much like a California onigiri, but made with poached shrimp instead of crab.

Yields: 6

Time: 30 minutes

Ingredients:

- Cooked Plain rice (1½ cups)
- Shrimp meat (6 oz., poached)
- Nori (2 sheets, roasted, halved)
- Avocado (1, cut into ½ inch slices)
- Cucumber (1, cut into ½ inch slices)
- Sesame Seeds (2 tbsp.)

Directions:

1. Combine shrimp meat, avocado, and cucumber.

2. Set your rice next to you, a second bowl next to it with salt, an empty bowl in front of you and finally another large bowl with water.

3. Add a heaping spoonful of rice to the empty bowl (as much as needed for the size of onigiri you want to achieve).

4. Dip your hands into your water bowl, then rub your wet hands with a dash of salt.

5. Press the serving of rice into your palm to create a small well.

6. Add in your fillings combined in step one, then push it lightly into the rice.

7. Form the rice into a ball of triangle (based on preference).

8. Wrap your onigiri with a strip of nori then dip into sesame seeds if you so desire or serve. Enjoy!

Seattle Onigiri

A delicious combination of cucumber, cream cheese, salmon, and avocado.

Yields: 6 pieces

Time: 30 minutes

Ingredients:

- Cooked Plain rice (1½ cups)
- Cucumber (4 oz., diced)
- Avocado (1/2, diced)
- Fresh Salmon (4oz., diced)
- Cream Cheese (2 tbsp., chopped)
- Nori (1 sheet, halved)
- Sesame Seeds (2 tbsp.)

Directions:

1. Combine salmon, cucumber, avocado, and cream cheese in a medium bowl.

2. Set your rice next to you, a second bowl next to it with salt, an empty bowl in front of you and finally another large bowl with water.

3. Add a heaping spoonful of rice to the empty bowl (as much as needed for the size of onigiri you want to achieve).

4. Dip your hands into your water bowl, then rub your wet hands with a dash of salt.

5. Press the serving of rice into your palm to create a small well.

6. Add in your fillings combined in step one, then push it lightly into the rice.

7. Form the rice into a ball of triangle (based on preference).

8. Wrap your onigiri with a strip of nori then dip into sesame seeds if you so desire or serve. Enjoy!

Smoked Salmon Onigiri

Add smoked salmon to your onigiri for a modern twist.

Yields: 6

Time: 30 minutes

Ingredients:

- Cooked Plain rice (1½ cups)
- Fresh Smoked salmon (6 oz., thinly sliced)
- Sesame Oil (2 tbsp.)

Directions:

1. Set your rice next to you, a second bowl next to it with salt, an empty bowl in front of you and finally another large bowl with water.

2. Add a heaping spoonful of rice to the empty bowl (as much as needed for the size of onigiri you want to achieve).

3. Dip your hands into your water bowl, then rub your wet hands with a dash of salt.

4. Press the serving of rice into your palm to create a small well.

5. Form the rice into a ball of triangle (based on preference).

6. Wrap your onigiri with a strip of smoked salmon then drizzle with sesame oil if you so desire or serve. Enjoy!

Teriyaki chicken Onigiri

A tasty combination of teriyaki chicken, nori, and Japanese rice.

Yields: 8 pieces

Time: 30 minutes

Ingredients:

- Cooked Plain rice (1½ cups)
- Teriyaki chicken (4 oz., minced)
- Sriracha Sauce (3 tsp.)
- Green Onion (1 tsp, chopped)
- Sesame Oil (1/2 tsp.)
- Nori (1 sheet, halved)
- Sesame Seeds (2 tbsp.)
- Spicy Mayo (optional for garnish/dipping)

Directions:

1. Combine teriyaki chicken, green onions, sesame oil, and sriracha sauce.

2. Set your rice next to you, a second bowl next to it with salt, an empty bowl in front of you and finally another large bowl with water.

3. Add a heaping spoonful of rice to the empty bowl (as much as needed for the size of onigiri you want to achieve).

4. Dip your hands into your water bowl, then rub your wet hands with a dash of salt.

5. Press the serving of rice into your palm to create a small well.

6. Add in your fillings combined in step one, then push it lightly into the rice.

7. Form the rice into a ball of triangle (based on preference).

8. Wrap your onigiri with a strip of nori then dip into sesame seeds if you so desire or serve. Enjoy!

Conclusion

Thank you so much for taking this journey through the world of Onigiri with me. I hope you enjoyed all 30 Modern Onigiri Recipe Twists featured in this Onigiri with a Twist Cookbook.

Please take a minute to leave me your feedback on Amazon so I can see what you thought of this book.

Enjoy your Onigiri!

About the Author

Born in New Germantown, Pennsylvania, Stephanie Sharp received a Masters degree from Penn State in English Literature. Driven by her passion to create culinary masterpieces, she applied and was accepted to The International Culinary School of the Art Institute where she excelled in French cuisine. She has married her cooking skills with an aptitude for business by opening her own small cooking school where she teaches students of all ages.

Stephanie's talents extend to being an author as well and she has written over 400 e-books on the art of cooking and baking that include her most popular recipes.

Sharp has been fortunate enough to raise a family near her hometown in Pennsylvania where she, her husband and children live in a beautiful rustic house on an extensive piece of land. Her other passion is taking care of the furry members of her family which include 3 cats, 2 dogs and a potbelly pig named Wilbur.

Watch for more amazing books by Stephanie Sharp coming out in the next few months.

Author's Afterthoughts

I am truly grateful to you for taking the time to read my book. I cherish all of my readers! Thanks ever so much to each of my cherished readers for investing the time to read this book!

With so many options available to you, your choice to buy my book is an honour, so my heartfelt thanks at reading it from beginning to end!

I value your feedback, so please take a moment to submit an honest and open review on Amazon so I can get valuable insight into my readers' opinions and others can benefit from your experience.

Thank you for taking the time to review!

Stephanie Sharp

For announcements about new releases, please follow my author page on Amazon.com!

You can find that at:

https://www.amazon.com/author/stephanie-sharp

*or Scan **QR-code** below.*

Printed in Dunstable, United Kingdom